SCHOOL TIMETABLE

MONDAY	TUESDAY	WEDNESDAY	THURSDAY	FRIDAY

TO-DO LIST

- ☐
- ☐
- ☐
- ☐
- ☐
- ☐
- ☐
- ☐
- ☐

SCHOOL
TIMETABLE

MONDAY	TUESDAY	WEDNESDAY	THURSDAY	FRIDAY

TO-DO LIST

- [ ]
- [ ]
- [ ]
- [ ]
- [ ]
- [ ]
- [ ]
- [ ]
- [ ]
- [ ]
- [ ]
- [ ]
- [ ]
- [ ]
- [ ]
- [ ]
- [ ]
- [ ]

SCHOOL TIMETABLE

MONDAY	TUESDAY	WEDNESDAY	THURSDAY	FRIDAY

TO-DO LIST

SCHOOL TIMETABLE

MONDAY	TUESDAY	WEDNESDAY	THURSDAY	FRIDAY

TO-DO LIST

SCHOOL TIMETABLE

MONDAY	TUESDAY	WEDNESDAY	THURSDAY	FRIDAY

TO-DO LIST

- ☐
- ☐
- ☐
- ☐
- ☐
- ☐
- ☐
- ☐
- ☐
- ☐
- ☐
- ☐
- ☐
- ☐
- ☐
- ☐
- ☐
- ☐

SCHOOL
TIMETABLE

MONDAY	TUESDAY	WEDNESDAY	THURSDAY	FRIDAY

TO-DO LIST

- [ ]
- [ ]
- [ ]
- [ ]
- [ ]
- [ ]
- [ ]
- [ ]
- [ ]
- [ ]
- [ ]
- [ ]
- [ ]
- [ ]
- [ ]
- [ ]
- [ ]
- [ ]

SCHOOL
TIMETABLE

MONDAY	TUESDAY	WEDNESDAY	THURSDAY	FRIDAY

TO-DO LIST

- ☐
- ☐
- ☐
- ☐
- ☐
- ☐
- ☐
- ☐
- ☐
- ☐
- ☐
- ☐
- ☐
- ☐
- ☐
- ☐

SCHOOL TIMETABLE

MONDAY	TUESDAY	WEDNESDAY	THURSDAY	FRIDAY

TO-DO LIST

- [ ]
- [ ]
- [ ]
- [ ]
- [ ]
- [ ]
- [ ]
- [ ]
- [ ]

- [ ]
- [ ]
- [ ]
- [ ]
- [ ]
- [ ]
- [ ]
- [ ]
- [ ]

SCHOOL TIMETABLE

MONDAY	TUESDAY	WEDNESDAY	THURSDAY	FRIDAY

TO-DO LIST

- [ ]
- [ ]
- [ ]
- [ ]
- [ ]
- [ ]
- [ ]
- [ ]
- [ ]

SCHOOL TIMETABLE

MONDAY	TUESDAY	WEDNESDAY	THURSDAY	FRIDAY

TO-DO LIST

SCHOOL TIMETABLE

MONDAY	TUESDAY	WEDNESDAY	THURSDAY	FRIDAY

TO-DO LIST

SCHOOL TIMETABLE

MONDAY	TUESDAY	WEDNESDAY	THURSDAY	FRIDAY

TO-DO LIST

SCHOOL TIMETABLE

MONDAY	TUESDAY	WEDNESDAY	THURSDAY	FRIDAY

TO-DO LIST

SCHOOL TIMETABLE

MONDAY	TUESDAY	WEDNESDAY	THURSDAY	FRIDAY

TO-DO LIST

SCHOOL TIMETABLE

MONDAY	TUESDAY	WEDNESDAY	THURSDAY	FRIDAY

TO-DO LIST

- ☐
- ☐
- ☐
- ☐
- ☐
- ☐
- ☐
- ☐
- ☐
- ☐
- ☐
- ☐
- ☐
- ☐
- ☐
- ☐

SCHOOL TIMETABLE

MONDAY	TUESDAY	WEDNESDAY	THURSDAY	FRIDAY

TO-DO LIST

- ☐
- ☐
- ☐
- ☐
- ☐
- ☐
- ☐
- ☐
- ☐
- ☐
- ☐
- ☐
- ☐
- ☐
- ☐
- ☐
- ☐
- ☐

SCHOOL TIMETABLE

MONDAY	TUESDAY	WEDNESDAY	THURSDAY	FRIDAY

TO-DO LIST

SCHOOL TIMETABLE

MONDAY	TUESDAY	WEDNESDAY	THURSDAY	FRIDAY

TO-DO LIST

SCHOOL TIMETABLE

MONDAY	TUESDAY	WEDNESDAY	THURSDAY	FRIDAY

TO-DO LIST

- ☐
- ☐
- ☐
- ☐
- ☐
- ☐
- ☐
- ☐
- ☐
- ☐
- ☐
- ☐
- ☐
- ☐
- ☐
- ☐

SCHOOL TIMETABLE

MONDAY	TUESDAY	WEDNESDAY	THURSDAY	FRIDAY

TO-DO LIST

- [ ]
- [ ]
- [ ]
- [ ]
- [ ]
- [ ]
- [ ]
- [ ]
- [ ]
- [ ]
- [ ]
- [ ]
- [ ]
- [ ]
- [ ]
- [ ]

SCHOOL TIMETABLE

MONDAY	TUESDAY	WEDNESDAY	THURSDAY	FRIDAY

TO-DO LIST

- [ ]
- [ ]
- [ ]
- [ ]
- [ ]
- [ ]
- [ ]
- [ ]
- [ ]
- [ ]
- [ ]
- [ ]
- [ ]
- [ ]
- [ ]
- [ ]

SCHOOL TIMETABLE

MONDAY	TUESDAY	WEDNESDAY	THURSDAY	FRIDAY

TO-DO LIST

- [ ]
- [ ]
- [ ]
- [ ]
- [ ]
- [ ]
- [ ]
- [ ]
- [ ]
- [ ]
- [ ]
- [ ]
- [ ]
- [ ]
- [ ]
- [ ]
- [ ]
- [ ]

SCHOOL TIMETABLE

MONDAY	TUESDAY	WEDNESDAY	THURSDAY	FRIDAY

TO-DO LIST

SCHOOL TIMETABLE

MONDAY	TUESDAY	WEDNESDAY	THURSDAY	FRIDAY

TO-DO LIST

SCHOOL
TIMETABLE

MONDAY	TUESDAY	WEDNESDAY	THURSDAY	FRIDAY

TO-DO LIST

SCHOOL TIMETABLE

MONDAY	TUESDAY	WEDNESDAY	THURSDAY	FRIDAY

TO-DO LIST

SCHOOL TIMETABLE

MONDAY	TUESDAY	WEDNESDAY	THURSDAY	FRIDAY

TO-DO LIST

- [ ]
- [ ]
- [ ]
- [ ]
- [ ]
- [ ]
- [ ]
- [ ]
- [ ]
- [ ]
- [ ]
- [ ]
- [ ]
- [ ]
- [ ]
- [ ]

SCHOOL TIMETABLE

MONDAY	TUESDAY	WEDNESDAY	THURSDAY	FRIDAY

TO-DO LIST

SCHOOL TIMETABLE

MONDAY	TUESDAY	WEDNESDAY	THURSDAY	FRIDAY

TO-DO LIST

SCHOOL
TIMETABLE

MONDAY	TUESDAY	WEDNESDAY	THURSDAY	FRIDAY

TO-DO LIST

SCHOOL TIMETABLE

MONDAY	TUESDAY	WEDNESDAY	THURSDAY	FRIDAY

TO-DO LIST

- ☐
- ☐
- ☐
- ☐
- ☐
- ☐
- ☐
- ☐
- ☐
- ☐
- ☐
- ☐
- ☐
- ☐
- ☐
- ☐

SCHOOL TIMETABLE

MONDAY	TUESDAY	WEDNESDAY	THURSDAY	FRIDAY

TO-DO LIST

- [ ]
- [ ]
- [ ]
- [ ]
- [ ]
- [ ]
- [ ]
- [ ]
- [ ]
- [ ]
- [ ]
- [ ]
- [ ]
- [ ]
- [ ]
- [ ]

SCHOOL TIMETABLE

MONDAY	TUESDAY	WEDNESDAY	THURSDAY	FRIDAY

TO-DO LIST

- [ ]
- [ ]
- [ ]
- [ ]
- [ ]
- [ ]
- [ ]
- [ ]
- [ ]
- [ ]
- [ ]
- [ ]
- [ ]
- [ ]
- [ ]
- [ ]

SCHOOL
TIMETABLE

MONDAY	TUESDAY	WEDNESDAY	THURSDAY	FRIDAY

TO-DO LIST

SCHOOL TIMETABLE

MONDAY	TUESDAY	WEDNESDAY	THURSDAY	FRIDAY

TO-DO LIST

- [ ]
- [ ]
- [ ]
- [ ]
- [ ]
- [ ]
- [ ]
- [ ]
- [ ]
- [ ]
- [ ]
- [ ]
- [ ]
- [ ]
- [ ]
- [ ]

SCHOOL TIMETABLE

MONDAY	TUESDAY	WEDNESDAY	THURSDAY	FRIDAY

TO-DO LIST

- [ ]
- [ ]
- [ ]
- [ ]
- [ ]
- [ ]
- [ ]
- [ ]
- [ ]
- [ ]
- [ ]
- [ ]
- [ ]
- [ ]
- [ ]
- [ ]
- [ ]
- [ ]

SCHOOL TIMETABLE

MONDAY	TUESDAY	WEDNESDAY	THURSDAY	FRIDAY

TO-DO LIST

- [ ]
- [ ]
- [ ]
- [ ]
- [ ]
- [ ]
- [ ]
- [ ]
- [ ]

SCHOOL TIMETABLE

MONDAY	TUESDAY	WEDNESDAY	THURSDAY	FRIDAY

TO-DO LIST

SCHOOL TIMETABLE

MONDAY	TUESDAY	WEDNESDAY	THURSDAY	FRIDAY

TO-DO LIST

- ☐
- ☐
- ☐
- ☐
- ☐
- ☐
- ☐
- ☐
- ☐
- ☐
- ☐
- ☐
- ☐
- ☐
- ☐
- ☐

SCHOOL TIMETABLE

MONDAY	TUESDAY	WEDNESDAY	THURSDAY	FRIDAY

TO-DO LIST

- ☐
- ☐
- ☐
- ☐
- ☐
- ☐
- ☐
- ☐
- ☐
- ☐
- ☐
- ☐
- ☐
- ☐
- ☐
- ☐
- ☐
- ☐

SCHOOL TIMETABLE

MONDAY	TUESDAY	WEDNESDAY	THURSDAY	FRIDAY

TO-DO LIST

- [ ]
- [ ]
- [ ]
- [ ]
- [ ]
- [ ]
- [ ]
- [ ]
- [ ]
- [ ]
- [ ]
- [ ]
- [ ]
- [ ]
- [ ]
- [ ]
- [ ]
- [ ]

SCHOOL TIMETABLE

MONDAY	TUESDAY	WEDNESDAY	THURSDAY	FRIDAY

TO-DO LIST

SCHOOL TIMETABLE

MONDAY	TUESDAY	WEDNESDAY	THURSDAY	FRIDAY

TO-DO LIST

- [ ]
- [ ]
- [ ]
- [ ]
- [ ]
- [ ]
- [ ]
- [ ]
- [ ]
- [ ]
- [ ]
- [ ]
- [ ]
- [ ]
- [ ]
- [ ]
- [ ]
- [ ]

SCHOOL TIMETABLE

MONDAY	TUESDAY	WEDNESDAY	THURSDAY	FRIDAY

TO-DO LIST

SCHOOL TIMETABLE

MONDAY	TUESDAY	WEDNESDAY	THURSDAY	FRIDAY

TO-DO LIST

- [ ]
- [ ]
- [ ]
- [ ]
- [ ]
- [ ]
- [ ]
- [ ]
- [ ]
- [ ]
- [ ]
- [ ]
- [ ]
- [ ]
- [ ]
- [ ]

SCHOOL TIMETABLE

MONDAY	TUESDAY	WEDNESDAY	THURSDAY	FRIDAY

TO-DO LIST

SCHOOL TIMETABLE

MONDAY	TUESDAY	WEDNESDAY	THURSDAY	FRIDAY

TO-DO LIST

- ☐
- ☐
- ☐
- ☐
- ☐
- ☐
- ☐
- ☐
- ☐
- ☐
- ☐
- ☐
- ☐
- ☐
- ☐
- ☐

SCHOOL TIMETABLE

MONDAY	TUESDAY	WEDNESDAY	THURSDAY	FRIDAY

TO-DO LIST

- ☐
- ☐
- ☐
- ☐
- ☐
- ☐
- ☐
- ☐
- ☐
- ☐
- ☐
- ☐
- ☐
- ☐
- ☐
- ☐

SCHOOL TIMETABLE

MONDAY	TUESDAY	WEDNESDAY	THURSDAY	FRIDAY

TO-DO LIST

- ☐
- ☐
- ☐
- ☐
- ☐
- ☐
- ☐
- ☐
- ☐
- ☐
- ☐
- ☐
- ☐
- ☐
- ☐
- ☐

SCHOOL
TIMETABLE

MONDAY	TUESDAY	WEDNESDAY	THURSDAY	FRIDAY

TO-DO LIST

SCHOOL TIMETABLE

MONDAY	TUESDAY	WEDNESDAY	THURSDAY	FRIDAY

TO-DO LIST

SCHOOL
TIMETABLE

MONDAY	TUESDAY	WEDNESDAY	THURSDAY	FRIDAY

TO-DO LIST

SCHOOL TIMETABLE

MONDAY	TUESDAY	WEDNESDAY	THURSDAY	FRIDAY

TO-DO LIST

- ☐
- ☐
- ☐
- ☐
- ☐
- ☐
- ☐
- ☐
- ☐
- ☐
- ☐
- ☐
- ☐
- ☐
- ☐
- ☐

SCHOOL TIMETABLE

MONDAY	TUESDAY	WEDNESDAY	THURSDAY	FRIDAY

TO-DO LIST

- ☐
- ☐
- ☐
- ☐
- ☐
- ☐
- ☐
- ☐
- ☐
- ☐
- ☐
- ☐
- ☐
- ☐
- ☐
- ☐
- ☐

SCHOOL TIMETABLE

MONDAY	TUESDAY	WEDNESDAY	THURSDAY	FRIDAY

TO-DO LIST

- ☐
- ☐
- ☐
- ☐
- ☐
- ☐
- ☐
- ☐
- ☐
- ☐
- ☐
- ☐
- ☐
- ☐
- ☐
- ☐

SCHOOL TIMETABLE

MONDAY	TUESDAY	WEDNESDAY	THURSDAY	FRIDAY

TO-DO LIST

- [ ]
- [ ]
- [ ]
- [ ]
- [ ]
- [ ]
- [ ]
- [ ]
- [ ]
- [ ]
- [ ]
- [ ]
- [ ]
- [ ]
- [ ]
- [ ]
- [ ]
- [ ]

SCHOOL TIMETABLE

MONDAY	TUESDAY	WEDNESDAY	THURSDAY	FRIDAY

TO-DO LIST

- ☐
- ☐
- ☐
- ☐
- ☐
- ☐
- ☐
- ☐
- ☐
- ☐
- ☐
- ☐
- ☐
- ☐
- ☐
- ☐
- ☐
- ☐

SCHOOL TIMETABLE

MONDAY	TUESDAY	WEDNESDAY	THURSDAY	FRIDAY

TO-DO LIST

- [ ]
- [ ]
- [ ]
- [ ]
- [ ]
- [ ]
- [ ]
- [ ]
- [ ]
- [ ]
- [ ]
- [ ]
- [ ]
- [ ]
- [ ]
- [ ]
- [ ]
- [ ]

SCHOOL TIMETABLE

|| MONDAY | TUESDAY | WEDNESDAY | THURSDAY | FRIDAY |

TO-DO LIST

- [ ]
- [ ]
- [ ]
- [ ]
- [ ]
- [ ]
- [ ]
- [ ]
- [ ]
- [ ]
- [ ]
- [ ]
- [ ]
- [ ]
- [ ]
- [ ]

SCHOOL TIMETABLE

MONDAY	TUESDAY	WEDNESDAY	THURSDAY	FRIDAY

TO-DO LIST

- [ ]
- [ ]
- [ ]
- [ ]
- [ ]
- [ ]
- [ ]
- [ ]
- [ ]
- [ ]
- [ ]
- [ ]
- [ ]
- [ ]
- [ ]
- [ ]
- [ ]
- [ ]

SCHOOL TIMETABLE

MONDAY	TUESDAY	WEDNESDAY	THURSDAY	FRIDAY

TO-DO LIST

- [ ]
- [ ]
- [ ]
- [ ]
- [ ]
- [ ]
- [ ]
- [ ]
- [ ]
- [ ]
- [ ]
- [ ]
- [ ]
- [ ]
- [ ]
- [ ]
- [ ]
- [ ]

SCHOOL TIMETABLE

MONDAY	TUESDAY	WEDNESDAY	THURSDAY	FRIDAY

TO-DO LIST

SCHOOL TIMETABLE

MONDAY	TUESDAY	WEDNESDAY	THURSDAY	FRIDAY

TO-DO LIST

- [ ]
- [ ]
- [ ]
- [ ]
- [ ]
- [ ]
- [ ]
- [ ]
- [ ]
- [ ]
- [ ]
- [ ]
- [ ]
- [ ]
- [ ]
- [ ]
- [ ]
- [ ]

SCHOOL TIMETABLE

MONDAY	TUESDAY	WEDNESDAY	THURSDAY	FRIDAY

TO-DO LIST

SCHOOL TIMETABLE

MONDAY	TUESDAY	WEDNESDAY	THURSDAY	FRIDAY

TO-DO LIST

- ☐
- ☐
- ☐
- ☐
- ☐
- ☐
- ☐
- ☐
- ☐
- ☐
- ☐
- ☐
- ☐
- ☐
- ☐
- ☐

SCHOOL TIMETABLE

MONDAY	TUESDAY	WEDNESDAY	THURSDAY	FRIDAY

TO-DO LIST

- [ ]
- [ ]
- [ ]
- [ ]
- [ ]
- [ ]
- [ ]
- [ ]
- [ ]
- [ ]
- [ ]
- [ ]
- [ ]
- [ ]
- [ ]
- [ ]
- [ ]
- [ ]

SCHOOL TIMETABLE

MONDAY	TUESDAY	WEDNESDAY	THURSDAY	FRIDAY

TO-DO LIST

- [ ]
- [ ]
- [ ]
- [ ]
- [ ]
- [ ]
- [ ]
- [ ]
- [ ]
- [ ]
- [ ]
- [ ]
- [ ]
- [ ]
- [ ]
- [ ]
- [ ]
- [ ]

SCHOOL
TIMETABLE

MONDAY	TUESDAY	WEDNESDAY	THURSDAY	FRIDAY

TO-DO LIST

SCHOOL TIMETABLE

MONDAY	TUESDAY	WEDNESDAY	THURSDAY	FRIDAY

TO-DO LIST

- ☐
- ☐
- ☐
- ☐
- ☐
- ☐
- ☐
- ☐
- ☐

SCHOOL TIMETABLE

MONDAY	TUESDAY	WEDNESDAY	THURSDAY	FRIDAY

TO-DO LIST

SCHOOL TIMETABLE

MONDAY	TUESDAY	WEDNESDAY	THURSDAY	FRIDAY

TO-DO LIST

SCHOOL TIMETABLE

MONDAY	TUESDAY	WEDNESDAY	THURSDAY	FRIDAY

TO-DO LIST

- [ ]
- [ ]
- [ ]
- [ ]
- [ ]
- [ ]
- [ ]
- [ ]
- [ ]
- [ ]
- [ ]
- [ ]
- [ ]
- [ ]
- [ ]
- [ ]
- [ ]
- [ ]

SCHOOL TIMETABLE

MONDAY	TUESDAY	WEDNESDAY	THURSDAY	FRIDAY

TO-DO LIST

- ☐
- ☐
- ☐
- ☐
- ☐
- ☐
- ☐
- ☐
- ☐
- ☐
- ☐
- ☐
- ☐
- ☐
- ☐
- ☐
- ☐
- ☐

SCHOOL TIMETABLE

MONDAY	TUESDAY	WEDNESDAY	THURSDAY	FRIDAY

TO-DO LIST

SCHOOL TIMETABLE

MONDAY	TUESDAY	WEDNESDAY	THURSDAY	FRIDAY

TO-DO LIST

- ☐
- ☐
- ☐
- ☐
- ☐
- ☐
- ☐
- ☐
- ☐
- ☐
- ☐
- ☐
- ☐
- ☐
- ☐
- ☐
- ☐
- ☐

SCHOOL TIMETABLE

MONDAY	TUESDAY	WEDNESDAY	THURSDAY	FRIDAY

TO-DO LIST

- [ ]
- [ ]
- [ ]
- [ ]
- [ ]
- [ ]
- [ ]
- [ ]
- [ ]
- [ ]
- [ ]
- [ ]
- [ ]
- [ ]
- [ ]
- [ ]
- [ ]
- [ ]

SCHOOL TIMETABLE

MONDAY	TUESDAY	WEDNESDAY	THURSDAY	FRIDAY

TO-DO LIST

- ☐
- ☐
- ☐
- ☐
- ☐
- ☐
- ☐
- ☐
- ☐

- ☐
- ☐
- ☐
- ☐
- ☐
- ☐
- ☐
- ☐
- ☐

SCHOOL TIMETABLE

MONDAY	TUESDAY	WEDNESDAY	THURSDAY	FRIDAY

TO-DO LIST

- [ ]
- [ ]
- [ ]
- [ ]
- [ ]
- [ ]
- [ ]
- [ ]
- [ ]
- [ ]
- [ ]
- [ ]
- [ ]
- [ ]
- [ ]
- [ ]
- [ ]
- [ ]

SCHOOL TIMETABLE

MONDAY	TUESDAY	WEDNESDAY	THURSDAY	FRIDAY

TO-DO LIST

- ☐
- ☐
- ☐
- ☐
- ☐
- ☐
- ☐
- ☐
- ☐
- ☐
- ☐
- ☐
- ☐
- ☐
- ☐
- ☐
- ☐
- ☐

SCHOOL TIMETABLE

MONDAY	TUESDAY	WEDNESDAY	THURSDAY	FRIDAY

TO-DO LIST

- ☐
- ☐
- ☐
- ☐
- ☐
- ☐
- ☐
- ☐
- ☐
- ☐
- ☐
- ☐
- ☐
- ☐
- ☐
- ☐
- ☐
- ☐

SCHOOL TIMETABLE

MONDAY	TUESDAY	WEDNESDAY	THURSDAY	FRIDAY

TO-DO LIST

- ☐
- ☐
- ☐
- ☐
- ☐
- ☐
- ☐
- ☐
- ☐

- ☐
- ☐
- ☐
- ☐
- ☐
- ☐
- ☐
- ☐
- ☐

SCHOOL TIMETABLE

MONDAY	TUESDAY	WEDNESDAY	THURSDAY	FRIDAY

TO-DO LIST

SCHOOL TIMETABLE

MONDAY	TUESDAY	WEDNESDAY	THURSDAY	FRIDAY

TO-DO LIST

SCHOOL TIMETABLE

MONDAY	TUESDAY	WEDNESDAY	THURSDAY	FRIDAY

TO-DO LIST

- [ ]
- [ ]
- [ ]
- [ ]
- [ ]
- [ ]
- [ ]
- [ ]
- [ ]
- [ ]
- [ ]
- [ ]
- [ ]
- [ ]
- [ ]
- [ ]
- [ ]
- [ ]

SCHOOL TIMETABLE

MONDAY	TUESDAY	WEDNESDAY	THURSDAY	FRIDAY

TO-DO LIST

SCHOOL TIMETABLE

MONDAY	TUESDAY	WEDNESDAY	THURSDAY	FRIDAY

TO-DO LIST

SCHOOL TIMETABLE

MONDAY	TUESDAY	WEDNESDAY	THURSDAY	FRIDAY

TO-DO LIST

- ☐
- ☐
- ☐
- ☐
- ☐
- ☐
- ☐
- ☐
- ☐

SCHOOL TIMETABLE

MONDAY	TUESDAY	WEDNESDAY	THURSDAY	FRIDAY

TO-DO LIST

- [ ]
- [ ]
- [ ]
- [ ]
- [ ]
- [ ]
- [ ]
- [ ]
- [ ]
- [ ]
- [ ]
- [ ]
- [ ]
- [ ]
- [ ]
- [ ]
- [ ]
- [ ]

SCHOOL TIMETABLE

MONDAY	TUESDAY	WEDNESDAY	THURSDAY	FRIDAY

TO-DO LIST

- ☐
- ☐
- ☐
- ☐
- ☐
- ☐
- ☐
- ☐
- ☐
- ☐
- ☐
- ☐
- ☐
- ☐
- ☐
- ☐
- ☐
- ☐

SCHOOL TIMETABLE

MONDAY	TUESDAY	WEDNESDAY	THURSDAY	FRIDAY

TO-DO LIST

SCHOOL TIMETABLE

MONDAY	TUESDAY	WEDNESDAY	THURSDAY	FRIDAY

TO-DO LIST

- [ ]
- [ ]
- [ ]
- [ ]
- [ ]
- [ ]
- [ ]
- [ ]
- [ ]
- [ ]
- [ ]
- [ ]
- [ ]
- [ ]
- [ ]
- [ ]
- [ ]
- [ ]

SCHOOL TIMETABLE

MONDAY	TUESDAY	WEDNESDAY	THURSDAY	FRIDAY

TO-DO LIST

- [ ]
- [ ]
- [ ]
- [ ]
- [ ]
- [ ]
- [ ]
- [ ]
- [ ]
- [ ]
- [ ]
- [ ]
- [ ]
- [ ]
- [ ]
- [ ]
- [ ]
- [ ]

SCHOOL TIMETABLE

MONDAY	TUESDAY	WEDNESDAY	THURSDAY	FRIDAY

TO-DO LIST

- ☐
- ☐
- ☐
- ☐
- ☐
- ☐
- ☐
- ☐
- ☐

- ☐
- ☐
- ☐
- ☐
- ☐
- ☐
- ☐
- ☐
- ☐

SCHOOL TIMETABLE

MONDAY	TUESDAY	WEDNESDAY	THURSDAY	FRIDAY

TO-DO LIST

SCHOOL TIMETABLE

MONDAY	TUESDAY	WEDNESDAY	THURSDAY	FRIDAY

TO-DO LIST

SCHOOL TIMETABLE

MONDAY	TUESDAY	WEDNESDAY	THURSDAY	FRIDAY

TO-DO LIST

- ☐
- ☐
- ☐
- ☐
- ☐
- ☐
- ☐
- ☐
- ☐
- ☐
- ☐
- ☐
- ☐
- ☐
- ☐
- ☐
- ☐
- ☐

SCHOOL TIMETABLE

MONDAY	TUESDAY	WEDNESDAY	THURSDAY	FRIDAY

TO-DO LIST

- [ ]
- [ ]
- [ ]
- [ ]
- [ ]
- [ ]
- [ ]
- [ ]
- [ ]
- [ ]
- [ ]
- [ ]
- [ ]
- [ ]
- [ ]
- [ ]

SCHOOL TIMETABLE

MONDAY	TUESDAY	WEDNESDAY	THURSDAY	FRIDAY

TO-DO LIST

SCHOOL TIMETABLE

MONDAY	TUESDAY	WEDNESDAY	THURSDAY	FRIDAY

TO-DO LIST

SCHOOL TIMETABLE

MONDAY	TUESDAY	WEDNESDAY	THURSDAY	FRIDAY

TO-DO LIST

- ☐
- ☐
- ☐
- ☐
- ☐
- ☐
- ☐
- ☐
- ☐
- ☐
- ☐
- ☐
- ☐
- ☐
- ☐
- ☐
- ☐
- ☐

SCHOOL TIMETABLE

MONDAY	TUESDAY	WEDNESDAY	THURSDAY	FRIDAY

TO-DO LIST

- ☐
- ☐
- ☐
- ☐
- ☐
- ☐
- ☐
- ☐
- ☐
- ☐
- ☐
- ☐
- ☐
- ☐
- ☐
- ☐

SCHOOL TIMETABLE

MONDAY	TUESDAY	WEDNESDAY	THURSDAY	FRIDAY

TO-DO LIST

- [ ]
- [ ]
- [ ]
- [ ]
- [ ]
- [ ]
- [ ]
- [ ]
- [ ]
- [ ]
- [ ]
- [ ]
- [ ]
- [ ]
- [ ]
- [ ]
- [ ]
- [ ]

SCHOOL TIMETABLE

MONDAY	TUESDAY	WEDNESDAY	THURSDAY	FRIDAY

TO-DO LIST

SCHOOL TIMETABLE

MONDAY	TUESDAY	WEDNESDAY	THURSDAY	FRIDAY

TO-DO LIST

- [ ]
- [ ]
- [ ]
- [ ]
- [ ]
- [ ]
- [ ]
- [ ]
- [ ]
- [ ]
- [ ]
- [ ]
- [ ]
- [ ]
- [ ]
- [ ]
- [ ]
- [ ]

SCHOOL TIMETABLE

MONDAY	TUESDAY	WEDNESDAY	THURSDAY	FRIDAY

TO-DO LIST

SCHOOL TIMETABLE

MONDAY	TUESDAY	WEDNESDAY	THURSDAY	FRIDAY

TO-DO LIST

- [ ]
- [ ]
- [ ]
- [ ]
- [ ]
- [ ]
- [ ]
- [ ]
- [ ]
- [ ]
- [ ]
- [ ]
- [ ]
- [ ]
- [ ]
- [ ]
- [ ]
- [ ]

SCHOOL TIMETABLE

MONDAY	TUESDAY	WEDNESDAY	THURSDAY	FRIDAY

TO-DO LIST

SCHOOL TIMETABLE

MONDAY	TUESDAY	WEDNESDAY	THURSDAY	FRIDAY

TO-DO LIST

- [ ]
- [ ]
- [ ]
- [ ]
- [ ]
- [ ]
- [ ]
- [ ]
- [ ]
- [ ]
- [ ]
- [ ]
- [ ]
- [ ]
- [ ]
- [ ]
- [ ]
- [ ]

SCHOOL TIMETABLE

MONDAY	TUESDAY	WEDNESDAY	THURSDAY	FRIDAY

TO-DO LIST

- [ ]
- [ ]
- [ ]
- [ ]
- [ ]
- [ ]
- [ ]
- [ ]
- [ ]
- [ ]
- [ ]
- [ ]
- [ ]
- [ ]
- [ ]
- [ ]
- [ ]
- [ ]

SCHOOL TIMETABLE

MONDAY	TUESDAY	WEDNESDAY	THURSDAY	FRIDAY

TO-DO LIST

SCHOOL TIMETABLE

MONDAY	TUESDAY	WEDNESDAY	THURSDAY	FRIDAY

TO-DO LIST

- [ ]
- [ ]
- [ ]
- [ ]
- [ ]
- [ ]
- [ ]
- [ ]
- [ ]
- [ ]
- [ ]
- [ ]
- [ ]
- [ ]
- [ ]
- [ ]
- [ ]
- [ ]

SCHOOL TIMETABLE

MONDAY	TUESDAY	WEDNESDAY	THURSDAY	FRIDAY

TO-DO LIST

SCHOOL TIMETABLE

MONDAY	TUESDAY	WEDNESDAY	THURSDAY	FRIDAY

TO-DO LIST

- ☐
- ☐
- ☐
- ☐
- ☐
- ☐
- ☐
- ☐
- ☐
- ☐
- ☐
- ☐
- ☐
- ☐
- ☐
- ☐
- ☐
- ☐

SCHOOL TIMETABLE

MONDAY	TUESDAY	WEDNESDAY	THURSDAY	FRIDAY

TO-DO LIST

- ☐
- ☐
- ☐
- ☐
- ☐
- ☐
- ☐
- ☐
- ☐
- ☐
- ☐
- ☐
- ☐
- ☐
- ☐
- ☐
- ☐
- ☐

SCHOOL TIMETABLE

MONDAY	TUESDAY	WEDNESDAY	THURSDAY	FRIDAY

TO-DO LIST

SCHOOL
TIMETABLE

MONDAY	TUESDAY	WEDNESDAY	THURSDAY	FRIDAY

TO-DO LIST

☐
☐
☐
☐
☐
☐
☐
☐
☐

☐
☐
☐
☐
☐
☐
☐
☐
☐

SCHOOL TIMETABLE

MONDAY	TUESDAY	WEDNESDAY	THURSDAY	FRIDAY

TO-DO LIST

- ☐
- ☐
- ☐
- ☐
- ☐
- ☐
- ☐
- ☐
- ☐

- ☐
- ☐
- ☐
- ☐
- ☐
- ☐
- ☐
- ☐
- ☐

SCHOOL TIMETABLE

MONDAY	TUESDAY	WEDNESDAY	THURSDAY	FRIDAY

TO-DO LIST

SCHOOL TIMETABLE

MONDAY	TUESDAY	WEDNESDAY	THURSDAY	FRIDAY

TO-DO LIST

- [ ]
- [ ]
- [ ]
- [ ]
- [ ]
- [ ]
- [ ]
- [ ]
- [ ]
- [ ]
- [ ]
- [ ]
- [ ]
- [ ]
- [ ]
- [ ]
- [ ]
- [ ]

SCHOOL TIMETABLE

MONDAY	TUESDAY	WEDNESDAY	THURSDAY	FRIDAY

TO-DO LIST